NO

MORE

DELAY

BISHOP KUNLE AMOO

Published by:

Best 'K' Books

In conjunction with:

Spectacle Prints and Digital Communication

Suite 11-14, Praise Plaza, Addo Road, Ajah, Lagos, Nigeria.

Telephone: +234(0)803 067 5056, +234(0)708 451 2745

Instagram: @spectacleprints

www.spectaclenigeria.com

ISBN: 978-978-979-904-6

CONTENTS

Introduction

I am delighted to finish his book in Jerusalem, the city of Israel, the holy land, the country of the birth of our lord Jesus Christ, whom I have given my life to and vowed episcopally and sacrificially to serve always. Delay is not a good thing in the life of all individuals. I have witnessed and overcome it many times in the past in ministry, marriage, career and business. You too can overcome it. You are actually an overcomer in Jesus name.

I believe as you read this spiritual book and diligently carry out the exercises at the end of the book for 7 days, delay will no longer be in your life or that situation, in Jesus name. I thank my wife and children, all my fathers and mothers in the Lord, minister colleagues, church members, friends and well-wishers, who gave me the chance and opportunities to write this book.

I thank Pastor Segun Akintoye MOE and his printing outfit for the quick publishing of this book.

"Not by might, nor by power, but by my spirit," *says the lord.*

Zechariah 4:6

Bishop Olukunle Olanrewaju Amoo JP PhD

1.30 am, 21 December, 2019.

Jerusalem, Israel

Foreword

My perusal through the book "No More Delay" by Bishop Olukunle Amoo came from ample years of practical Ministry of the word and counseling from various people of different backgrounds and cultures.

Delay is not synonymous to perseverance either from theological or anthropological point of view.

The point at which the writer is looking at subject matter shows that DELAY does not primarily come from God Almighty, but as a result of certain occurrences of life and events which does not imply the fact God cannot overrule the spirit behind delay in our lives and families.

If someone has ever experienced delay ,such will never pray for its repeat in his life or even his enemy because the aftermath of delay usually cause an unprecedented setbacks and unlimited liabilities.

The goodnews is that the journey of delay can be overcomed and broken finally if we are able to cry to the " Author and Finisher" of our life and faith. Moreover, precautionary measures must be taken humanly to avert the causes of delay in all ramifications of our life.

I wish you the very best as you meticulously read this inspired book of this humble servant of God. For there shall be No More delay in Jesus name.

Rt Revd Ambassador Davies T.O.Faleye (MEWN, FCMA, JP)

The Presbyterian Church of Nigeria. Abeokuta Parish

+234-806-760-0985

PROLOGUE

No More Delay

I am writing basically on demonic delays. When a four-year-old child cannot walk or talk, we know something is wrong medically or spiritually.

May I say that everything that happened or is happening to a man has a foundation in the spirit realm. It later always manifests physically or medically. The spiritual dictates the physical, whether financially, socially or medically.

God never planned for any mortal to be stagnant or to be a failure. Everything God made is always perfect. In fact, God took a nice holiday after He had worked, and perfected everything that concerns human beings after the 6th day. On the

7th day, God had a nice rest. Exodus 31: 17 says God was refreshed.

Exodus 31:17

It will be a sign between me and the Israelites forever, for in six days the LORD made the heavens and the earth, and on the seventh day he rested...

During those six days, nothing delayed the ability of God.

Genesis 2:2.

Thus the heavens and the earth were finished, and all the host of them.And on the seventh day God ended his work which he had made...

My prayer for the reader of this book is that by the time you finish this book and specifically the exercises at the last pages, nothing shall delay your prayers again, in the mighty name of Jesus.

You won't witness any form of delay again. Never ever! No More delay In Jesus Mighty Name.

CHAPTER 1

IS THIS DELAY FROM GOD

Daniel 10:12-13 King James Version (KJV)

12 Then said he unto me, Fear not, Daniel: for from the first day that thou didst set thine heart to understand, and to chasten thyself before thy God, thy words were heard, and I am come for thy words.

13 But the prince of the kingdom of Persia withstood me one and twenty days: but, lo, Michael, one of the chief princes, came to help me; and I remained there with the kings of Persia.

I can understand a person who misses a flight because of an impending air crash; this can be attributed to an act of God. But I cannot understand a person who has a delay for further studies because he could not pass a particular examination after some six attempts! The latter is not likely to be a delay from God. Something is likely to be responsible!

Causes of delays:

1. Sin
2. Lack of seriousness
3. Demonic attack

Chapter 2

SIN

Sin is a break in relationship with God. Our first physical father, Adam, disobeyed God with Eve and the consequence was physical death for all mankind. If not, it would have been a rosy and cozy non-ending enjoyment for all mankind in the garden of Eden and in life generally.

 But sin broke that covenant with God. Since sin brought struggles to Adam and Eve, they genetically passed the struggles generationally to all mankind. Thank God for Jesus Christ who came to give us a second chance. Halleluiah!

Genesis 3 King James Version (KJV)

3 *Now the serpent was more subtil than any beast of the field which the Lord God had made.*

And he said unto the woman, Yea, hath God said, Ye shall not eat of every tree of the garden?

2 And the woman said unto the serpent, We may eat of the fruit of the trees of the garden:

3 But of the fruit of the tree which is in the midst of the garden, God hath said, Ye shall not eat of it, neither shall ye touch it, lest ye die.

4 And the serpent said unto the woman, Ye shall not surely die:

5 For God doth know that in the day ye eat thereof, then your eyes shall be opened, and ye shall be as gods, knowing good and evil.

6 And when the woman saw that the tree was good for food, and that it was pleasant to the eyes, and a tree to be desired to make one wise, she took of the fruit thereof, and did eat, and gave also unto her husband with her; and he did eat.

7 And the eyes of them both were opened, and they knew that they were naked; and they sewed fig leaves together, and made themselves aprons.

8 And they heard the voice of the LORD God walking in the garden in the cool of the day: and Adam and his wife hid themselves from the presence of the LORD God amongst the trees of the garden.

9 And the LORD God called unto Adam, and said unto him, Where art thou?

10 And he said, I heard thy voice in the garden, and I was afraid, because I was naked; and I hid myself.

11 *And he said, Who told thee that thou wast naked? Hast thou eaten of the tree, whereof I commanded thee that thou shouldest not eat?*

12 *And the man said, The woman whom thou gavest to be with me, she gave me of the tree, and I did eat.*

13 *And the LORD God said unto the woman, What is this that thou hast done? And the woman said, The serpent beguiled me, and I did eat.*

14 *And the LORD God said unto the serpent, Because thou hast done this, thou art cursed above all cattle, and above every beast of the field; upon thy belly shalt thou go, and dust shalt thou eat all the days of thy life:*

15 *And I will put enmity between thee and the woman, and between thy seed and her seed; it shall bruise thy head, and thou shalt bruise his heel.*

[16] *Unto the woman he said, I will greatly multiply thy sorrow and thy conception; in sorrow thou shalt bring forth children; and thy desire shall be to thy husband, and he shall rule over thee.*

[17] *And unto Adam he said, Because thou hast hearkened unto the voice of thy wife, and hast eaten of the tree, of which I commanded thee, saying, Thou shalt not eat of it: cursed is the ground for thy sake; in sorrow shalt thou eat of it all the days of thy life;*

[18] *Thorns also and thistles shall it bring forth to thee; and thou shalt eat the herb of the field;*

[19] *In the sweat of thy face shalt thou eat bread, till thou return unto the ground; for out of it wast thou taken: for dust thou art, and unto dust shalt thou return.*

Before, all Adam needed to do to feed was to pluck a fruit and eat, now he had to weed, cut, plough and farm and "wait" for the fruits to be harvested. Sin postpones miracles and eventually hinders answers to prayers. Sin doesn't make God to open the heavens on any individual that lives a life of constant disobedience.

Romans 6: 1-18 King James Version (KJV)
6 What shall we say then? Shall we continue in sin, that grace may abound?

2 God forbid. How shall we, that are dead to sin, live any longer therein?

3 Know ye not, that so many of us as were baptized into Jesus Christ were baptized into his death?

4 Therefore we are buried with him by baptism into death: that like as Christ was raised up from the dead by the glory of the Father, even so we also should walk in newness of life.

⁵ For if we have been planted together in the likeness of his death, we shall be also in the likeness of his resurrection:

⁶ Knowing this, that our old man is crucified with him, that the body of sin might be destroyed, that henceforth we should not serve sin.

⁷ For he that is dead is freed from sin.

⁸ Now if we be dead with Christ, we believe that we shall also live with him:

⁹ Knowing that Christ being raised from the dead dieth no more; death hath no more dominion over him.

¹⁰ For in that he died, he died unto sin once: but in that he liveth, he liveth unto God.

11 Likewise reckon ye also yourselves to be dead indeed unto sin, but alive unto God through Jesus Christ our Lord.

12 Let not sin therefore reign in your mortal body, that ye should obey it in the lusts thereof.

13 Neither yield ye your members as instruments of unrighteousness unto sin: but yield yourselves unto God, as those that are alive from the dead, and your members as instruments of righteousness unto God.

14 For sin shall not have dominion over you: for ye are not under the law, but under grace.

15 What then? Shall we sin, because we are not under the law, but under grace? God forbid.

16 Know ye not, that to whom ye yield yourselves servants to obey, his servants ye are to whom ye obey; whether of sin unto death, or of obedience unto righteousness?

17 But God be thanked, that ye were the servants of sin, but ye have obeyed from the heart that form of doctrine which was delivered you.

18 Being then made free from sin, ye became the servants of righteousness.

People that live in sin sometimes have favour and grace withdrawn from them. Those individuals don't usually measure up with their counterparts in life. When as adults, they should be riding a car, they will find it difficult to buy a bicycle tyre.

Every act of disobedient makes God look away and allows or enemies to pursue us.

Deuteronomy 31:6

6 Be strong and of a good courage, fear not, nor be afraid of them: for the LORD thy God, he it is that doth go with thee; he will not fail thee, nor forsake thee.

Is it easy to live a sinless life? This is a very good question. Those who do not lie or commit adultery, but have evil thoughts in their minds, have sinned. Those who insult or discourage or look down on their fellow human beings, who made in the image of God, have not done well. Consistently, we all fall into some errors, either small or big. Sin is sin. That is why Jesus, in The Lord's Prayer, taught us to ask our heavenly Father for forgiveness of our sins.

Matthew 6:9-13 King James Version (KJV)
⁹ After this manner therefore pray ye: Our Father which art in heaven, Hallowed be thy name.

10 Thy kingdom come, Thy will be done in earth, as it is in heaven.

11 Give us this day our daily bread.

12 And forgive us our debts, as we forgive our debtors.

13 And lead us not into temptation, but deliver us from evil: For thine is the kingdom, and the power, and the glory, forever. Amen.

We have a sure way to God to receive forgiveness for any sin we have committed. God is also able to cleanse us from all unrighteousness. And whoever God has cleansed is clean.

1 John 1:8-9

If we say that we have fellowship with him, and walk in darkness, we lie, and do not the truth:

7 But if we walk in the light, as he is in the light, we have fellowship one with another, and the blood of Jesus Christ his Son cleanseth us from all sin.

8 If we say that we have no sin, we deceive ourselves, and the truth is not in us.

9 If we confess our sins, he is faithful and just to forgive us our sins, and to cleanse us from all unrighteousness.

10 If we say that we have not sinned, we make him a liar, and his word is not in us.

Whoever God has not condemned can never be detained or delayed. Do you have a delay in one or two areas of your life? You need to reflect on your life. If there is a sin you consistently commit, why can't you confess that sin right now, then forsake it TOTALLY? If you do so, you will find out that very soon that delay will be no more, in Jesus Name. You are free from the bondage of sin.You are free from any delay associated with disobedience in Jesus name. You have been set free... Receive God's speed of accomplishment, in Jesus name.

John 8:36

[36] **If the Son therefore shall make you free, ye shall be free indeed.**

Chapter 3

BE SERIOUS

Many people live a carefree life, secularly and spiritually. Attitude determines altitude.

Whenever there is a challenge in life, the next task is to overcome that challenge. Winners of today refused to quit yesterday. They saw failure but refused to accept it. I want you to refuse delay as your position in life. Whether in academics, in marriage or in career, delay is not your friend. It's an enemy that must be defeated. Never treat delay with kid's glove.

Romans 12:3-11 New King James Version (NKJV)

3 For I say, through the grace given to me, to everyone who is among you, not to think *of himself* more highly than he ought to think,

but to think soberly, as God has dealt to each one a measure of faith. ⁴ For as we have many members in one body, but all the members do not have the same

function, ⁵ so we, *being* many, are one body in Christ, and individually members of one another. ⁶ Having then gifts differing according to the grace that is given to us, *let us use them:* if prophecy, *let us prophesy* in proportion to our faith; ⁷ or ministry, *let us use it* in *our* ministering; he who teaches, in teaching; ⁸ he who exhorts, in exhortation; he who gives, with liberality; he who leads, with diligence; he who shows mercy, with cheerfulness.

⁹ *Let* love *be* without hypocrisy. Abhor what is evil. Cling to what is good. ¹⁰ *Be* kindly affectionate to one another with brotherly love, in honor giving preference to one

another; [11] not lagging in diligence, fervent in spirit, serving the Lord;

Those who will overcome any form of delay will leave no stone unturned but will do all that is necessary to get the obstacle away.

1 Cor 9:24

Do you not know that those who run in a race all run, but one receives the prize? Run in such a way that you may obtain it.

Heb 12:2

Looking unto Jesus, the author and finisher of *our* faith, who for the joy that was set before Him endured the cross, despising the shame, and has sat down at the right hand of the throne of God.

Jesus didn't care about the issues, noises and shame that happened before and during his crucifixion. He had his goal and vision in mind. He even refused to listen to the armed robber who was who was also on the cross beside him.

Can you kindly be serious physically and spiritually and be deaf to all noises about your present circumstances and focus on your destination? Your destiny is secured and you're a champion in Jesus Name!

I had been a Pastor to a couple who, for 22 years, had believed God for children. They had tried everything possible. I had the privilege to counsel them one Sunday after church service and in the course of the counseling, I asked each of them what the challenges were. The man said there was no problem. The wife looked at him and said, "Pastor there are issues!" Openly, we discussed the problem and I told the wife there was no problem. God can solve it. And God did solve it. They were given some spiritual exercises, as well as some physical and medical examinations. Also, I gave them some daily prayer points and encouraged them to get involved in Kingdom service. I also told them to be truthful to themselves with personal evaluations. They should also try and stay focused by avoiding noises and distractions from friends and relatives offering them any ungodly counsel.

God gave them twins, a boy and a girl, on October 4, 2018, after 22 years of waiting. To God be the glory! The wife mentioned one thing of note. She said in all the churches they had been attending prior to joining our church, once the husband was given a kingdom service, that would be the last day they would worship in that church. However, when he became active as church secretary and a member of Treasury, God

rewarded him. Please be serious! You are serious
in Jesus Name.

Hebrew 11: 6

**But without faith *it is* impossible to
please *Him,* for he who comes to God must
believe that He is, and *that* He is a rewarder of
those who diligently seek Him.**

Chapter 4

NO MORE COMPLAINTS

I knew a sister that always asked me, "Daddy in the Lord..." "God is our Daddy," I always corrected. She would continue, "When will God answer this 21 years prayer point of mine?" She had always asked me this question since we first met and I had become her Pastor. I noticed her prayer points were always with complaints; she would always start with grumblings. Up till now, God has not answered her prayer point. I've counseled her to leave complaints and ask God nicely. We ask God some requests poorly than we can ask our bosses at work. We address God casually and we worship our bosses, mentors and godfathers. How I wish we could respect the Immortal God more than a human being who is temporal and mortal. Some of us insult God with our prayer requests in the manner and approach. It is well with us, in Jesus name.

1 Corinthians 10:10

Nor complain, as some of them also complained, and were destroyed by the destroyer.

May God grant us wisdom to remove complaints from our prayer requests, in Jesus name.

Chapter 5

DEMONIC ATTACK

Due to family backgrounds like polygamy, jealousy and strife have caused damages to destinies that should be continuously progressive.

The older wife would not want the children of the youngest wife to make progress in life and vice versa. Every evil arrow from polygamous settings that has caused delay into your life and destiny is cancelled, in Jesus name. I cancel that arrow out of your destiny by FIRE!

Most children from polygamous marriages suffer from emotional and spiritual problems that follow them into adulthood, their marriages and career. A young man was inflicted with infertility by his mother's rival who mopped the young man's urine with a cloth and TOOK IT TO A HERBALIST. He could not impregnate any woman until he was delivered. Every attack from the person that hates your mother that has caused any delay in your life, that attack is removed in Jesus name.

> Demonic attacks from a polygamous linage is evil and you are free from it, in Jesus name.

Ephesians 6:12

For we do not wrestle against flesh and blood, but against the rulers, against the authorities, against the cosmic powers over this present darkness, against the spiritual forces of evil in the heavenly places.

Many have suffered afflictions from evil-minded neighbors or co-workers, envious friends and relatives and have had their destinies tampered with. I have good news for you today if you are demonically attacked or being continuously attacked – every evil arrow fired by demonic agents are sent back to sender by fire in Jesus name. Receive your freedom this hour in Jesus name!

Every demonic agent and diviners used to afflict you (if you can say a loud Amen) are powerless in your life, in Jesus name. Divine freedom is your heritage, in Jesus Name.

John 8:36

So if the Son sets you free, you will be free indeed.

Chapter 6

IDOL WORSHIPPING FAMILY
Joshua 24:2

And Joshua said to all the people, "Thus says the LORD God of Israel: 'Your fathers, including Terah, the father of Abraham and the father of Nahor, dwelt on the other side of [a]the River in old times; and they served other gods...

Many Africans and North American homes, who are today Christians, were once Idol worshipers. Idolatry is gravely frowned and detested God. Many were masquerades worshipers, many worshipped gods of iron and thunder, in fact, many have murdered human beings and used their blood for rituals. Blood speaks, as we saw in Cain and Abel's issue.

Cain was a wanderer because of that murderous act. If your destiny is wandering or roaming about because of murder, hunger or idolatry, you are delivered today, in Jesus name.

People from masquerade-worshipping families oftentimes are hindered from timely marriage. They are either always dumped or never see a spouse to marry. Masquerades are scary and their crowns and robes are dirty and with bad odour; who would marry a masquerade? Every offensive and scary spirit delaying your marital progress is sent into bondage, in Jesus name.

Some people from idol worshipping backgrounds are always offensive to their benefactors or helpers. The spirit that has denied you breakthrough is leaving your life right now, in Jesus Name.

Whoever you are or wherever you are and you are reading this book and you've not seen a spectacular breakthrough in life and you know your ancestors were idolatry, please shout, "The blood of Jesus." seven times! And say, "I am cleansed." three times. Say, "I dissociate myself from every ancestral idol, in Jesus name." You are delivered, in Jesus name.

Until Abram dissociated from his kinsmen of idolatory worshipers in Tehran, his life was in shambles, he never had a change of name and status, He was not progressive or rich and the promises of God was never fulfilled in his life.

Gen 12:1

Now the LORD had said to Abram:

"Get out of your country,
From your family

And from your father's house,

To a land that I will show you.

He became Abraham, he was a father of many nations and he was extremely rich. Can you once again shout with Holy anger three times, "I DISSOCIATE MYSELF FROM MY IDOLATORY ANCESTORS BY FIRE IN JESUS NAME"? AMEN and FIRE!

You are extremely wealthy in Jesus name. Kindly pray it many times and confess the scripture below. You are Rich! Amen!

Genesis 13:2 Abram was very rich in livestock, in silver, and in gold.

Sickness or delay in healing is peculiar to some families because of the covenant their forefathers had with some idols. They must not use hot water to bathe or eat some particular types of food.

Every bondage of delayed healing is cancelled in Jesus Name. Every bondage of sickness is broken. Periodical or seasonal sicknesses shall never be your portion again, in Jesus Mighty name.

Isaiah 53:5 But he was wounded for our transgressions, he was bruised for our iniquities: the chastisement of our peace was upon him; and with his stripes we are healed.

From today, enjoy uncommon divine health in Jesus name I declare!

Demonic attacks on careers and businesses are also common among brethren and unbelievers. Unexplained non-promotion at work or profitless businesses can be linked to occultic covenants by forefathers who have sacrificed the future of their unborn generations on evil altars. Every evil altar speaking failure to your destiny, may fire consume that altar completely in Jesus Name.

Demonic attacks are also possible through dreams. Many people have been afflicted through evil dreams. A lady suddenly got knocked off by a bike at a bus stop one day. Immediately, she shouted and said, "I saw this accident in a dream yesterday. Jesus! I saw it o." That was an affliction in the dream.

Matthew 13:25-30

25 but while men slept, his enemy came and sowed tares among the wheat and went his way. 26 But when the grain had sprouted and produced a crop, then the tares also appeared. 27 So the servants of the owner came and said to him, 'Sir, did you not sow good seed in your field? How then does it have tares?' 28 He said to them, 'An enemy has done this.' The servants said to him, 'Do you want us then to go and gather them up?' 29 But he said, 'No, lest while you gather up the tares

you also uproot the wheat with them. [30] Let both grow together until the harvest, and at the time of harvest I will say to the reapers, "First gather together the tares and bind them in bundles to burn them, but gather the wheat into my barn."

Every dream-acquired yokes are broken in your life, in Jesus name. Dreams of snails, seeing red objects, being pursued by masquerades, giving birth, having sexual intercourse, eating demonic foods, etc., are evil yokes against productive destinies.

Some have eaten demonic meals and they become sick, got hooked to hospital beds and delayed from progress with daily activities hindered. Every delay acquired by evil dreams are broken, in Jesus Name.

Chapter 7

SALVATION

Delay is not denial, I agree, but then it is better to do good things of life quickly than to wait for years before they are achieved. You won't be delayed again in life, in Jesus name.

However, the salvation of our souls is important than any miracle on planet Earth. Before you pray the next 7 daily hot prayers against delay, I would like to invite you to come to Jesus, the Savior of the world. Without Christ, it is a life of crisis. It is easy to come to Jesus, He has paid that price on the cross of Calvary. Friend, I invite you to say the following prayers of salvation with me:

"Dear Lord Jesus Christ, I repent of all sins I have committed knowingly or unknowingly. Release mercy and grace to me henceforth. I accept you as my Lord and Savior. I confess

that Jesus is the son of God. Help me to live a good Christian life and enable me to be your working ambassador on earth. So help me God. AMEN"

Very simple indeed! Welcome friend! We are now brothers and sisters in the Lord. Please attend a Bible-based church, preaching the word of God in your area.

You can now FREELY and BOLDLY pray the 7 days hot deliverance prayer to overcome delay.

Freely because **John 8:36** says, **"Therefore if the Son makes you free, you shall be free indeed."**

Boldly because **Hebrews 4:16** says, **"Let us therefore come boldly to the throne of grace, that we may obtain mercy and find grace to help in time of need."**

Remember the two verses of the Bible constantly, "Freely" John 8:36 and "Boldly" Hebrews 4:16. Delay is no more your portion, in Jesus name. You have overcome delay permanently. Henceforth, live a life of constant favour and receive God's speed in all your endeavors, in Jesus name. Let us look at the following inspirational verses also:

Romans 8:37 *Yet in all these things we are more than conquerors through Him who loved us.*

Genesis 6:8 But Noah found grace in the eyes of the LORD

Proverb 8:35 for whoever finds me finds life,And obtains favor from the LORD;

Luke 2:52 And Jesus increased in wisdom and stature, and in favor with God and Men.

You are anointed for favours and breakthroughs over delays, in Jesus Mighty name. AMEN!

Shalom!

Chapter 8

7 DAYS HOT PRAYER POINTS TO CANCEL EVIL DELAYS

Pray each prayer daily, with accompanying Bible verses and fasting till 3pm or 6pm as you are able, unless it is contrary to medical advice.

I recommend that you pray this prayer daily and repeatedly for 15 minutes at 6am, 9am, 12noon, 3pm, 6pm, 9pm and 12am. Reading loud the scriptures and praying it with holy anger! Always shout, "Blood of Jesus" seven times and "Holy Ghost Fire" seven times at the beginning and end of each prayer session. You will share your testimony with a new song, in Jesus name.

Day 1:

Every roots of delay in my life, dry up by fire!

Job 18:16: His roots are dried out below and his branch withers above.

Day 2:

Arrows of delay fired into my life, fly out by fire!

Jeremiah 30:16-17:[16] 'Therefore all those who devour you shall be devoured. And all your adversaries, every one of them, shall go into captivity;Those who plunder you shall become plunder,

And all who prey upon you I will make a prey.
[17] For I will restore health to youAnd heal you of your wounds,' says the LORD,'Because they called you an outcast *saying:*
"This *is* Zion;No one seeks her." '

Day 3:

My stolen star, Arise and Shine!

Isaiah 60:1Arise, shine;

For your light has come!

And the glory of the LORD is risen upon you.

Day 4:

Ancestral yokes delaying my breakthroughs,
break by fire!
John 8:36: so if the Son sets you free, you will be
free indeed.

Day 5:

Demonic influence on my destiny, be cast out,
in Jesus name. Come out, in Jesus name! Pray
it in a loud voice!

Acts 8:7: For unclean spirits, crying out with a loud voice, came out of many who had them, and many who were paralyzed or lame were healed.

Day 6:

I receive the anointing of good life; I receive the anointing of good health; I receive the anointing of power over demonic delay, in Jesus name.

Acts 10:38: How God anointed Jesus of Nazareth with the Holy Spirit and with power. He went about doing good and healing all who were oppressed by the devil, for God was with him.

Day 7:

I cancel all curses working with delays against my life by fire!

Galatians 3:13: Christ has redeemed us from the curse of the law, having become a curse for us (for it is written, "Cursed *is* everyone who hangs on a tree").